Towards the Holy Spirit

PHILIP TOYNBEE

Towards the Holy Spirit

SCM PRESS LTD

334 01693 2

This edition first published 1982
by SCM Press Ltd, 58 Bloomsbury Street, London

Photoset by John Smith, London
and printed in Great Britain by
Richard Clay (The Chaucer Press) Ltd
Bungay, Suffolk

CONTENTS

INTRODUCTION

It seems almost presumptuous to intrude on this classically simple, closely argued, tersely expressed and yet extremely personal book. However, because the unusual and perhaps forbidding format does not immediately indicate just what is to be found in *Towards the Holy Spirit*, those coming to it for the first time may find a few comments and words of explanation useful. For here, still in as tantalizingly fragmentary form as Dietrich Bonhoeffer's *Letters and Papers from Prison*, is one of the great spiritual documents of the twentieth century.

In 1973, the late Ivan Yates, at that time Religious Affairs Correspondent of *The Observer*, came to SCM Press with a rather battered manuscript which was causing problems. It was by Philip Toynbee, who reviewed regularly for *The Observer*, and it was too long for a newspaper article and too short, really, to make a book. What was to be done? I had read one piece of Philip Toynbee's writing previously which had made a very deep impression on me: an assessment of Karl Barth, written after Barth's death in 1968, which seemed to me to come closer to recognizing Barth's real significance than most of what had been written by professional theologians. So I took the manuscript, read it avidly several times – and we had to publish it. Our compromise format, one of the most elegant pieces of typography we have produced, made a distinguished cased book of unusual shape, and at the same time must have limited the readership. Nevertheless, this 'Tract for the Times', as it was originally sub-titled, found a significant readership, and in conversation I have discovered that more than one eminent theologian regards it as a second Bible.

After publication of *Towards the Holy Spirit*, Philip Toynbee seemed to relapse into silence on religious matters; in fact over this period he was going through a devastating depression. But then, in mid-1978, came another memorable piece: an article, first published in *Encounter*, entitled 'Evensong at Peterborough', in part a sympathetic and vivid critique of the present ethos of the Church of England as exemplified in the activity which gives the article its name, and in part a continuation of the style of writing to be found in *Towards the Holy Spirit*. Because the second half fits so well with the earlier book (though as a result of the passage of time and Philip Toynbee's further reflections there are obvious points of tension), it is reprinted here. The title, 'A Marriage of Heaven and Earth', is that of a book he once hoped that he would write.

From then until his death in the summer of 1981 I remained in contact with Philip Toynbee. We had hoped at one time to produce a collection of essays, centred on 'Evensong at Peterborough', which was making a deep impression on others who had discovered it, but sadly that never came to anything. What did appear, however, in 1981 was an autobiographical journal, *Part of a Journey*, published by Collins, which contained both 'Evensong at Peterborough' and another important lecture, 'Christianity and the Modern World', which he gave to the annual meeting of the General Assembly of Unitarian and Free Christian Churches (remarking, as he completed the draft: 'I suspect that those Unitarians are going to find me sadly credulous; even superstitious. For I doubt whether most of them believe even in one God by now.' And he was right. When he went up to Manchester to deliver the talk, 'one fat, elder-

2

ly and very robust minister from Massachusetts expressed surprise and dismay at my belief in God, in spite of the fact that my God is strictly unitarian. After a few minutes' discussion I asked him how he differed from Bertrand Russell. "Not very much. Not at all, in fact." '). *Part of a Journey* is a crucial companion to, and commentary on, *Towards the Holy Spirit*, though the important passages have to be dug out of a good deal of less impressive material. Most of the published reviews of the journal were so preoccupied with the way in which Philip Toynbee's concern for honesty led him to extensive and vivid confessions of failings that they missed the other side of it altogether, or dismissed it too hastily.

But why should Philip Toynbee claim attention in connection with religion and theology? The eulogistic adjectives have been brought out; what justifies them?

First and foremost, he could talk and write about theology without making a fool of himself. That is not a common gift. It is as difficult for anyone without formal theological training, not working among other theologians, to make a meaningful contribution to the discussion of contemporary problems as it is for, say, someone without training to make a worthwhile contribution to discussions about music – and for similar reasons. But Philip Toynbee had a clear eye for the issues, and while there are many points on which one might want to argue with him, he seems to me to have had his priorities right.

So secondly, he was deeply concerned with God. In the preface to his journal he describes how for the first fifty years of his life he remained 'in a fluctuating attitude of hostile fascination towards all forms of religious belief'. Then, perhaps influenced among other things by the conversion of his wife Sally to the Church of England (he had

3

already had a teenage shock when his mother became a Roman Catholic), 'one day, for no special reason that I was able to detect, I made what seemed like a final decision that I too believed in God, and was therefore ready to start examining all the religious knowledge I had acquired over the years, not just as an intellectual curiosity but as the possible approach to a livable reality' – though he did not become an Anglican!

The God in whom Philip Toynbee came to believe was a God of a stature to put alongside the God of Karl Barth, as was already clear in his memorial article on earth. He violently rejected any attempts to bring God down to man's level, as is clear from his comments on the use of the phrase 'the depth of our being':

> The form of 'belief' which makes God 'the depth of our being', etc., is simply old Atheism writ large. Religious trappings, the mutilation of religious language, make it all the worse. If they are anything at all these people are florid psychologists; anthropocentrics who fill out that empty centre with the language of profundity (*Part of a Journey*, p. 41).

Hence his scathing comment about his Unitarian audience. 'If,' he wrote later, 'it were irrefutably demonstrated to me that there is no God, and no reality above or distinct from the material world, then I would consider that human life is too terrible to endure.'

He was well aware of the problems, as the present book shows. In particular, he showed a realization of the challenge posed to Christianity by Buddhist spirituality, that debate of which, at the time I write this, Don Cupitt's book *Taking Leave of God* (SCM Press 1980) has become the focal point.

4

What does seem plain to me is that in our time the real challenge to a thinking Christian comes, not from his non-believing friends and associates – humanists; atheists; agnostics, whatever they call themselves – but from the more tough-minded forms of Buddhism ... Buddhists use the words 'holy' and 'sacred' with every bit as much confidence as Christians do; and no open-minded Christian could possibly deny the term 'holy' to a Truly Enlightened Buddhist. Yet this experience – of joy; of peace; of deep understanding – leads the Buddhist to quite different conclusions from the Christian's. He is not aware of a loving God penetrating his soul with light: for him the light comes solely from within himself; from the depths of his own being.

The challenge is formidable. The difference between the two religions is very deep. Contrast the sublime calm of the Buddha seated in meditation with the contorted Jesus on the cross (pp. 113f.).

What makes Philip Toynbee so aware of the conflict and contrast between Christianity and Buddhism is not just the question of the reality of God, but above all his own deep ethical concern. And that is his third great strength. It is the blandness of Buddhism which he cannot take, the serene indifference to the hungry and the destitute. One of the most moving passages in the journal is a reflection on a paragraph from Kierkegaard's *Journals* which pictures the way of tribulation in terms of a child in a dark room, waiting for the door to be opened and all the hoped-for glory, in the warmth and love of his parents, to be revealed, waiting and fearing right until the very last moment that he may have been forgotten and abandoned. 'It is also possible that at the last moment we too shall be crying, "My God, my God, why hast thou forsaken me!" And it is possible that even when we cry out like this on the point of death we shall believe that God hears our cry with deep love and a pain which is even greater than our own' (p. 354). The question of pain and suffering and evil and the sheer extent of it is never far away, often on the verge of tipping the fragile balance in the direction of despair and meaninglessness.

And then, among the pain and questioning, another note appears, as it does so often in his writing: a note of confident assertion.

All this talk of God 'including within himself' both good and evil; darkness and light. This sounds dramatic, sophisticated, even impressive so long as you stick to the grand abstractions. Let them come down to earth; tell us that God worked through Himmler just as surely as through St Francis. And what about the sheer squalor, meanness, *meagreness* of everyday vanity, greed, jealousy, malice. Are these as godlike as the life and death of Dietrich Bonhoeffer? (pp. 41f.)

Time and again the 'and yet ...' keeps reappearing in different guises. But there is always a conflict, a struggle, both intellectually and psychologically. The confident assertion is followed by another question; the elation and sense of assurance is followed by the depths of depression. For Philip Toynbee faith is not only a journey, but a struggle, in which we can never be too 'hot for certainty', never claim too much, never be over-confident. For if 'faith' is a moral quality (p. 48), in this world it can never escape sore trial, even when it seems impregnable (p. 260). No wonder he quotes Simone Weil:

There are three mysteries, three incomprehensible things in the world. Beauty, justice and truth.

6

They are the three things recognized by all men as standards for everything in the world. The incomprehensible is the standard for the known.

What wonder if terrestrial life is impossible? (p. 225)

And, in his own words, 'if to be in Heaven is to love as fully as possible then it is hard to see how pain could be banished so long as any suffering creature remains in any place' (p. 114).

And so, lastly, we come to the person of the man himself, through whom all this profound reflection is expressed. This is not the place for a rounded portrait of him, which in any case I am not competent to produce. But accept the blemishes, the excesses, the failings, for we all have them in more or less spectacular degree, and see the important characteristic, struggling to become more of the whole man: the pilgrim.

Conscious of the pressure of sceptics and unbelievers, and the stridency of those who thought they had the truth, he remarked, 'Always remember that the realistic alternative is not a man who claims to know the truth about Heaven, but a man who believes that there is such a truth, however little of it he knows. Or is ever likely to know.' He was aware of the telling arguments of psychologists against religion, but turned it back on them: 'It's true that the need is no proof that God exists; but it is at least a suggestive and interesting element in many people's compositions. Strange creatures, if we felt so strong a need for something which was never there.' Yet he doesn't know where it comes from. He is quick to say that his 'conversion' to believe in God was so unsensational, so undramatic, that he doubts whether he should use the word at all. He has never felt it possible to pray to Jesus; never felt the faintest flicker of his presence. So is the grace of God working imperceptibly within him? Or is the mind having its own way, constructing new patterns of belief according to its own chosen rules; a preposterous intellectual advance into a vacuum?

There is no answer. Only a hope. And let Philip Toynbee put that hope in his own way:

> I recognize more and more that if I have any godly function on earth – and of course I have; everybody has – then it is to act as both a warning and an example on the very lowest rungs of the ladder. The present account of my hopes and fears; large failures, small successes; humiliations and perceptions (perceptions often from the heart of humiliation) is meant for the spiritually backward – who nevertheless know enough about the Spirit to be in a state of often subdued but never extinguished hope (p. 337).

John Bowden
January 1982

Towards the Holy Spirit

A Tract for the Times

'Negative Capability, that is, when a man is capable of dealing in uncertainties, mysteries, doubts, without any irritable reaching after fact and reasoning . . .' KEATS

NOTE

This tract is not, and could not have been, a technically expert contribution either to theology or to philosophy, but it is meant to be as far away as possible from the whole area of personal confession or apologia. Although I hold the beliefs and attitudes which are expressed here, I have tried to present them in the form of a normative and impersonal statement from which others may take their departure in different directions.

Indeed in any confessional sense I am unusually ill-equipped for describing religious experience: I have had little, if any, of my own. But I have been deeply interested in the religious reports and interpretations of others from a very early age.

There are other limitations to my capacities and my achievements of which I am, I hope, as conscious as I ought to be. The first is that this is a very *English* treatise, written almost entirely within the ambience of recent Anglo-Saxon philosophy and theology. Either through ignorance or through lack of sympathy I have said nothing at all about that whole wide area of continental thought and sensibility which is evoked by the word 'Existentialism'. A writer must use what instruments he has, and do his limited best with them.

Finally this is, of course, a disputatious, even a polemical document. All I can say is that I have tried to be fair to those with whom I differ; though they are most unlikely to think that I have tried hard enough. I hope I may at least have stimulated them to answer back.

ONE

Doubts and Uncertainties

1 If we think hard enough in any single direction we always arrive at the unthinkable.

2 If we ask enough questions along a given line of enquiry we come in the end to an unanswerable question.

3 And this happens to all of us – scientists, philosophers, theologians and amateur thinkers – whatever our preconceptions and whatever final truth we had set out to prove or show.

4 We go on asking the forbidden questions in spite of the old warnings from the old myths: Eve; Pandora; Faust; and in spite of the agile mockery of certain modern philosophers: 'metaphysics' (with a hiss); 'nonsense-questions'; 'the ghost in the machine'.

5 What is new in the situation is that confidence has been partially eroded in every camp: the old assurance that all the answers have already been given (orthodox theology) or that all the answers will very soon be discovered (orthodox scientific materialism) has been replaced by a common condition of increasing doubt and bewilderment: even of humility: even of self-mockery.

6 What has happened is that hard-thinking men are beginning to conceive that a great deal of reality may be inconceivable by the human mind.

7 They have begun to suspect that the circle of human understanding within which we act and think may not, after all, be indefinitely expandable by scientific discovery or already fully illuminated by theological description. What lies about us is not so much the as-yet-unexplored as the inherently unexplorable. (Except, of course, for an indefinite but limited nimbus.)

8 If it is true that we are therefore in a mood of unusual intellectual humility then we may also be in an unusually good position to think again about what we think.

9 It might be said that the Hundred Year War between science and religion is at last beginning to peter out.

10 At first it would seem that this war has been virtually won by science, and that the forces of religion are in a state of unconcealed demoralization.

11 Their latest and longest retreat has been marked by the emergence of those who describe themselves as Christians, yet eagerly announce not only that God is dead – a hundred years after the news was given to the world by Nietzsche – but that the whole concept of the supernatural must now be abandoned.

12 It seems to be still assumed that scientists have 'discovered' or 'proved' that the natural order is the only real order. But how can any discipline which limits itself, by its own definition, to a given field of experience make any pronouncement at all on whether there are other fields of experience outside its own?

13 What *has* been effectively destroyed, partly by scientific discoveries but even more by a notable sharpening of historical awareness, is the whole traditional apparatus of Christian theology.

14 We should be able to understand, in our time, how the astonishingly complex and contorted dogmas of early Christianity were gradually evolved and contrived during the first four centuries after Christ.

15 We may – we ought to – admire, sympathize with and benefit from that tremendous work of intellectual elaboration and reconciliation; but how can we share either the modes of thought of St Paul and the Fathers or their confidence in the ability of man to people the unknown with such elaborate extensions of the known?

16 Not only are we under no obligation to believe in the Trinity, the resurrection of the body and the procession of the Holy Ghost; we are under the strictest obligation to say that this kind of language no longer has any use or meaning for us.

17 But underneath these exhausted minutiae of traditional Christian theology lies a far more profound and dignified assumption about the nature of reality; namely, that the universe was created by, and is sustained by, a God who is all-powerful, all-knowing and all-loving.

18 By far the heaviest blow to orthodox Christianity has been modern man's growing inability to accept the existence of such a God.

19 And the reason for this reluctant retreat from the most comforting of all beliefs is not 'scientific' or 'technological'; still less 'materialist'. The deeper reason is that there has been a drastic change in the nature and the operation of our moral sensibility.

20 We have become more sensitive to the evil of cruelty than any historical epoch has ever been before us. (Just as we have become far more morally obtuse in other areas.)

21 For us cruelty is the cardinal sin: just as pride was the cardinal sin for traditional Christianity.

22 And it is surely clear that the moral disposition of a society is as much an instrument of perception as any other: we 'see' with our eyes and our minds, but also with our hearts.

23 Contemplate, for a moment, a single 'act of God': there has been an earthquake, and in a young family of three the father has been killed at once; the mother dies, in noisy anguish, during the next twenty-four hours; the child, pinned down uninjured between his dead parents, dies slowly of thirst during the next five days, while the bodies of his parents putrefy to each side of him.

24 Modern Christians have devoted a great deal of hard and painful thought, a great many contorted and embarrassed pages, to finding excuses for such behaviour on the part of their all-loving and all-powerful God. (But why do they still call it the problem of evil rather than the problem of pain?

Because they still cling to the absurd and obsequious device of trying to blame man even for his own suffering. Yet the ludicrous contraption known as 'the Fall' does nothing whatever to absolve their God from the wickedness of his initial creation and continuing misconduct in the world.)

25 Every justification of God's ways to man proposes some covert and glorious end which more than atones for the overt and outrageous means. But it is among our sharpest moral perceptions that not even the most superb end can justify such means as the killing of this child in those circumstances.

26 (The notion of a God who is all-powerful *but evil* is a patently frivolous one: for whatever else a modern God may be, he must betoken, represent, embody an extrapolation of our highest perceptions and deepest moral convictions.)

27 (Another strategy of the Christians is to mutter the word 'mystery' whenever they are cornered. It is the principal contention of this tract that we are indeed surrounded by mysteries: but it also our plain disputational duty to use the word only as a term of last resort. And there is a resort beyond the use of the word at this point; namely to admit that nothing compels us to postulate an all-powerful God of love.)

28 To compress this overwhelming moral argument against the Christian God we might say that the recent sharpening of an ancient Judaeo-Christian moral perception has come

into increasing conflict with the Judaeo-Christian belief in a God who is both all-powerful and all-loving.

29 Love has finally banished the God of Love.

30 If we now turn our eyes away from the disarray of the Christians and observe the new uncertainties among their traditional opponents, it must be said at once that the present confusion among positivists has been due even less to successful operations by the forces of religion than Christian embarrassment has been caused by the assaults of science.

31 It is *wholly* because of developments within their own disciplines that many scientists and positivist philosophers have begun to talk in more hesitant terms than those they were using thirty years ago.

32 Thirty years ago leading British philosophers were condemning as 'literal nonsense' not only any proposition which is in plain contradiction with the accepted laws of linguistic usage but also any which is not capable of being either verified or falsified, at least 'in principle'.

33 At the same time the majority of scientists were still hoping that they could keep their already-ballooning hypotheses tethered, however remotely, to the accepted conventions of common sense.

34 In fact just as the theologians were offending against the positivist criterion of meaning by making assertions which

defied the verification principle ('God is Love'), so the physicists were already in gross contravention of common sense as the term is normally used and understood. They spoke of a universe which is (*a*) finite but unconfined, and (*b*) expanding, but expanding into nothing. They also told us that electrons are capable of passing through space without taking any time to do so.

35 Why, then, did the Logical Positivists constantly deride the 'nonsense' of religious discourse but say little if anything about the even more flagrant 'nonsense' of the physicists?

36 But since that time tough-minded philosophers, who would once have refused even to describe themselves as atheists (on the grounds that you cannot proclaim your disbelief in 'abracadabra') have had to retire from the patent absurdity of claiming that large areas of ordinary human conversation are literally nonsensical.

37 What many of them are now saying is that almost all forms of current usage must be held to make sense of a kind, and that the principal function of the modern philosopher is to elucidate the precise nature of this sense.

38 Meanwhile the physicists, forced to retreat from the confidence of their Victorian predecessors that science is nothing other than an indefinite application of the principles of common sense, have been obliged to talk 'nonsense' of a more and more extravagant kind.

39 They are now maintaining that a certain particle is able to

pass, in its undivided state, through two different holes at the same time.

40 They are postulating certain large 'holes in the sky' into which time and space not only disappear but in which they actually cease to be.

41 They are now proposing to make use of the term 'quark' to describe a particle of which the essential property is that when three of them combine, their collective weight is less than that of any one of them by itself; *although nothing has been lost by their conjunction.*

42 (When Dr Johnson kicked the stone, and proclaimed that he was demonstrating 'thus' the simple reality of the physical world, he was attempting to refute – though in fact grossly misunderstanding – the arguments of idealist philosophy. Today, in his role as champion of common sense, his action would presumably be an attempted refutation of atomic physics [the notion that the apparent solidity of objects is an illusion created by particles in constant and rapid motion]. Needless to say, Johnson's new 'demonstration' would be as foolish as the old one.)

43 The usual reply of scientists to charges that they are talking nonsense is to claim that their hypotheses cannot be intelligibly presented in ordinary language, but only by mathematical symbols which would mean nothing to the rest of us. But the reply of the cornered theologian was of much the same kind: he would retreat, under rationalist attack, into a protective smoke-screen of 'ineffables' and

'unutterables' and 'transcendentals', assuring his opponent that ordinary words can never do justice to the infinite mystery of God.

44 No sensible layman can simply 'reject' the 'nonsense' of the modern physicists: we are bound to recognize that these clever and passionately truthful men are doing their best to tell us about experiences which they have undergone in their laboratories and observatories. (Just as the early theologians were doing their best to interpret certain new types of religious experience.)

45 All we can say, at this point, is that physicists and astronomers seem to have been forced, by their recent observations, to certain baffling, absurd, contradictory, even 'impossible' conclusions about the nature of physical reality. We must register that at this point, and this one, and this one, physics seems to have reached the limit of what the human mind is able to describe, understand or even conceive of.

46 Anglo-American philosophers, too, have lost the almost apocalyptic confidence of thirty years ago; and the assurance that every traditional problem has either been solved or shown to be a pseudo-problem begins to seem almost touchingly simple-minded.

47 For example Professor Ryle's behaviourist – and derisively self-confident – dismissal of the whole mind-and-body problem ('the ghost in the machine') seems to have had strangely little staying power.

48 We continue to be exercised by our inability to reconcile our consciousness of freedom as an immediate experience with the impeccable philosophical demonstration that every event is determined. And the same stubborn persistence is shown by nearly all the other old philosophical enigmas.

49 Recent English and American philosophers – recent linguists from all over the world – have indeed done us the immense service of making us pay due attention to the linguistic element in every form of human communication. Their service has been one of clarification.

50 But far from old problems having been solved, or even successfully shelved, the truth seems to be that new enigmas are constantly being added to the ancient stock-pot by the increasingly sophisticated observations of the scientists.

51 As they make further observations on the sub-atomic and the super-stellar levels, scientists are finding far more new questions than new answers.

52 (You cannot ask what a quasar is, and how such a thing could possibly be, until you have been forced to confront the phenomena which demand that this new sort of question should be asked.)

53 Indeed it is remarkable that scientists gaily continue to ask themselves exactly the sort of question which many philosophers have tried, for so many years, to rule out of court as illegitimate and nonsensical.

54 Gauguin and his mournful Tahitians were not the last to ponder the antique question of origins.

55 The argument about beginnings ('Genesis myths') is now being vigorously conducted between two rival schools of astronomers. Some suggest that suddenly, a long time ago, something began where/when there had been nothing before (the theory of the 'big bang'). The others argue that, on the contrary, matter has always been creating itself out of nothing; that it continues to do so now, and that it will continue to do so for ever and ever (the 'steady state' theory).

56 But both these answers are not only nonsensical by any criterion of permissible linguistic usage; they are also, and by the same token, quite beyond the capacity of any human mind to encompass.

57 But we can reach this bounding-line of the humanly-conceivable from an even earlier point in the history of human thought.

58 It is maintained, in any secular-materialist theory of origins, that the whole process of creation and evolution has taken place autonomously: by the working of purely 'natural' causes. That is to say, by certain mathematically demonstrable laws of chance and probability.

59 But this seems to imply a proposition which is even more overtly nonsensical than any that has been already considered. For does it make any sense, outside Wonderland, to say that a windmill has changed into yesterday afternoon?

60 Yet the assertion that a ball of flaming gas has produced, or changed into, or evolved to make possible, the philosophy of Plato, is every bit as nonsensical as the above proposition.

61 Normally rigorous minds have been deceived into this gross confusion of incompatible linguistic categories by the sheer *length of time* which this change of matter into mind is supposed to have entailed. But whether the change is 'quick' or 'slow' according to our own arbitrary standards of time, it is clear that the linguistic absurdity remains.

62 (Nor does it help to suggest that the concept of mind is itself an illusory and confused one. It is still our – resolutely Cartesian – experience that we think that we think with rather more conviction than we think anything else.)

63 What this section has hoped to show is that we are living in a period when both sides in the major metaphysical disputation of our time ought to be feeling unusually chastened and open-minded.

64 Christians should recognize not only that their traditional theology was the very peculiar product of a very peculiar historical period; but also that their Creator-God of Love is no longer a morally acceptable hypothesis.

65 Scientists should recognize that they have been forced to confront phenomena which they can describe only in terms at least as repulsive to common sense as any that were ever used by Christian theologians.

26

66 Positivist philosophers should recognize not only that they have failed to make linguistic sense of recent scientific discoveries – although this was their overt declaration of intent thirty years ago – but also that most of the traditional philosophical puzzles have been neither solved nor shelved.

TWO

Mysteries

67 In any contemporary dispute between naturalists and supernaturalists it should be accepted, by a preliminary understanding, that we are all empiricists now.

68 The argument is not between those who confine themselves to the reality of human experience and those who do not; it is an argument about how best – most convincingly and most usefully – to interpret *the whole* of human experience.

69 (In fact, of course, even the old doctrine of special revelation had to base itself on a revelation made to men.)

70 Any examination of ordinary human speech will show that it is only on specialized occasions that words are used as a means of appealing to that common human faculty which we call 'reason'. The normal use of words implies an appeal to some assumed or hoped-for common ground of experience: 'It was like this for me. And for you?'

71 Thus the usual type of reply is not, 'Yes, my calculations agree with yours' (or, 'No, they do not'), but, 'Yes, your words adequately convey to me' (or, 'No, they fail to convey to me') 'that you have had an experience which resembles one of my own.'

72 There is a large, though vague and ill-defined, area of

experience which has always proved recalcitrant to any simple or naturalistic explanation.

73 A short list of common but intractable words may suggest the sort of experience which is now to be discussed: identity, language, love, beauty, freedom, art, death, beginning and end, truth, time, space, vision, the universe, infinity, eternity ...

74 These words do not suggest to us a vocabulary of un-solved problems; they seem to register something more than certain all-too-familiar exacerbations of the analysing mind. They sound to us more like the signs of ancient mysteries; they reverberate with a natural echo; they fill us with awe.

75 Examine, within this area of the well-known but mysterious, certain rare but universally recognized types of human behaviour.

76 An atheist, who is wholly convinced that his death will mean the total obliteration of his mind and body, sacrifices his life to save the life of another man in circumstances such that he cannot expect anyone else to be aware of his action. (He believes, in other words, that no posthumous credit will ever accrue to him, either in heaven or on earth.)

77 Another man, no less a disbeliever than the first either in God or in survival, chooses to be burned alive rather than abjure his beliefs. He does so although he is well aware that this martyrdom will be unknown to anybody

except his – plainly impermeable and un-communicative – executioners. It is therefore very improbable that his brave and defiant death will serve as an example or an encouragement to anybody else.

78 A man of the same disbeliefs who has been abandoned on a desert island chooses to die 'well' – that is to say, with calmness and dignity – under the empty sky.

79 A man who has always been known for the cynical worldliness of his actions and overt beliefs suddenly falls into a state of passionate but unrequited love. He immediately sacrifices his whole career, reputation and fortune in what he knows to be a hopeless pursuit of the beloved.

80 A man long habituated to a life of greed, lust, anger and brutal selfishness suddenly undergoes a conversion and becomes loving towards his fellows even to the point of ready and continual self-sacrifice.

81 Whenever we confront these forms of human behaviour, and the many others which resemble them, our first reaction is one of awe and amazement. (And this is the case even if we quickly suppress this emotion in favour of some rationalistic explanation.)

82 But in order to find what we are now looking for – namely, forms of human experience which are hard to explain as the satisfaction of obvious natural needs or impulses – it is not at all necessary to look so far.

83 It is universally accepted that some men have a more acute perception than others of their immediate physical environment. It is equally agreed that for all men the acuteness of their perceptions varies significantly at different times of day, or year, or life, or health.

84 But it is also a common, almost a universal, experience that we sometimes become the beneficiaries (or victims) of sudden and apparently inexplicable enhancements of our normal perceptions and apprehensions.

85 On a particular morning we wake up to an immediate sense of intensified awareness: the sky, the houses, the street, the people are perceived with a startling clarity – as if we had quite failed to see them clearly during our normal condition of muffled perceptiveness.

86 This abnormal acuteness of perception is often accompanied by a strong sense that the perceiver is looking *through* the natural objects about him.

87 That poets and artists are a special kind of men who undergo this experience in a different sort of way from other people may well be doubted. But we cannot doubt that such men have reported on their experiences with the special eloquence, vividness and enthusiasm of their chosen métier.

88 The intensity with which poets and artists have described their moments of special enlightenment have had little to do with their own metaphysical ambience. Paul

Valéry, one of the most intellectually austere and sceptical of poets, has spoken of instants when objects ceased to be signs to him and became *significances*.

89 (In spite of his passion for the precise and the explicit, Valéry left his strange word hanging in the air: he never ventured to say *what it was* that these objects signified.)

90 The most familiar cause of this reported hyper-perception is the experience known as 'falling in love'. According to a great many recorded reports this experience is accompanied by – is indeed signalized by – the trans-figuration of the beloved into a being of superlative beauty, charm, goodness ... In many cases the lover feels that he, too, has been elevated, transported, glorified. In some cases the whole surrounding world of man and nature undergoes a similar transformation.

91 The same kind of experience is constantly reported by those who have been deeply moved by looking at a picture, reading a poem, listening to music or visiting some scene of great natural beauty.

92 Those who take drugs also report that they have under-gone a sharp increase in the apparent acuteness of their perceptions. (It is irrelevant, at this point, to discuss the comparative value of such experiences. All that needs to be said here is that these different kinds of experience form a significant area of reported apprehension to which any conscientious empiricist must pay the most careful and thoughtful attention.)

93 A sense of the holiness of certain places has sometimes overwhelmed even the most impregnable of rationalists.

94 Immediate awareness of the holiness of certain people has been at least as frequent an experience among many who would be reluctant to find any meaning at all in the word 'holy'.

95 There are moments when we have the sense that everything which comes to our attention is trying to convey a message to us.

96 Observed from as far outside our own species as we can ever contrive to perch ourselves, it surely seems to us that man is not at home in his natural environment as a sea-snail, for example, is perfectly adapted to its own conditions.

97 Out of his evident contingency man constantly yearns for some being whose essence is to be not contingent but necessary; not relative but absolute.

98 Out of partiality man craves for totality.

99 Again and again man feels himself to be a mortal creature with immortal longings; a creature which constantly aspires far beyond any apparent capacity to satisfy his aspirations.

100 There are two distinct but associated factors which seem to unite all these different types of familiar experience.

The first is that they are accompanied by a strong sense of value *as something given and directly apprehended*. The experiences are felt both to *be* good and to be *of* the Good.

101 It is also a frequent conviction of those who have had such experiences that they have encountered something more than a mere sharpening of their normal senses. It is commonly reported that there has been a momentary apprehension of something *beyond* the phenomenal order of natural objects.

102 But there is, of course, a much rarer but reportedly an infinitely more intense and valued form of the visionary experience: this is the phenomenon known as mysticism.

103 It is an odd and perhaps a disquieting fact that this always-awkward topic has been largely ignored during the last twenty years, not only by sceptical materialists but also by the dominant apologists for some form of attenuated religious faith. (Yet there has been a significant and increasing, though rather vague and confused, interest in mystical experience among young people.)

104 If this is a period when some scientists are beginning to suspect that there is more in heaven and earth than was dreamed of in their previous philosophy, it is also a period when Christians are readily admitting that there is a great deal less – of the definable and the describable – than their own philosophy had contrived to elaborate. Yet few scientists and positivists have yet been willing to pay any serious attention to mystical experience, while most Christian

apologists have treated it as that part of their traditional cargo which can most easily be jettisoned.

105 (A slightly ludicrous metaphor presents itself: just as the Christians are making breathlessly for that shore from which the seemingly well-planted positivists used to mock them, the positivists, finding that the shore is dissolving under their feet, have begun to take their first few tentative steps into the breakers.)

106 Thus mystical experience, so much in vogue twenty to thirty years ago, has become a source of some embarrassment in these days of hesitant rapprochement between the articulate proponents of Christianity and 'humanism'.

107 It would be absurd, in this place, to provide yet another précis of the reports delivered by those who claim to have had mystical experience.

108 But there are certain facts to be re-established; and the first of them is that a very high proportion of the men and women who have laid claim to this order of experience were renowned in their daily lives for probity, charity *and good sense*. There have also, of course, been lunatics and charlatans among them, but it is certain that the great body of mystical *writing* which has survived is the work of human beings of exceptional repute and credibility.

109 What we have here, in fact, is a large body of reported experience from the best of all possible human sources – many of them saints, not only by canonization but by any

reputable criterion of human excellence. And what those persons are telling us is that this particular experience has been incomparably the most valuable and the most significant that they have ever known.

110 It is notorious, of course, that the language which mystics habitually use is one of extreme paradox, of elevated vagueness, of large and loose words piled dizzily on top of each other; or of everyday and precise words used only to construct what must appear to most non-mystics to be the most extravagant of metaphors.

111 But if these experiences are utterly remote from those for which ordinary language was devised, it is not in the least surprising that ordinary language should have proved inadequate to describe them.

112 In any case, there are at least two declarations which emerge with perfect clarity and intelligibility from all the written and spoken words of the reputable mystics.

113 The first is this: the mystics believe themselves to have encountered an order of reality which is utterly distinct, though not, of course, discrete, from the phenomenal world of the senses. They are persuaded that this is not merely an episode, or idiosyncrasy, or exaltation within their own minds, but a reality which exists quite independently of those who experience it.

114 The second universal report is that this order of reality is infinitely superior, by every accepted criterion of value, to anything the mystics have ever encountered in their

ordinary lives. It is, they tell us, more joyful; more beautiful; infinitely more deeply suffused with love, wisdom and hope. They even tell us that it is more *real*.

115 (And is there, by way of afterthought, *nothing* that deserves the attention of an honest observer in all that wide *demi-monde* of ghosts and mediums, of hauntings and premonitions? Is there nothing worth looking at in all those proceedings of societies for psychical research; in all those strange and laborious statistics compiled by departments of paranormal psychology? Anyone who has tried to make an unprejudiced study of these goings-on – both the respectable and the not-so-respectable – must surely have concluded that there are signs and mysteries here which deserve better than the kind of *a priori* hatred and contempt which they have all too often received from self-styled empiricists.)

116 And, in this context, what a pleasure it would be to read a proper study of that fascinating figure, the semi-charlatan: the man or woman who belongs, for most of his time and through most of his nature, so dingily and shamelessly to this world, but who seems, through no very evident merit, to be also endowed with fitful powers of *genuine* vision and understanding. (There are plenty of back-passages and curious by-ways for the entry of the mysterious into the natural world. It is not always a glorious business or even a creditable one.)

117 The problem, in any case, is how to account for – or at least how to regard – all this strange patchwork of reported experience – culminating in the great corpus of mystical

writing. How should we react to the suggestion that human beings can sometimes penetrate the world of the senses and encounter a reality which lies beyond it?

THREE

Irritable Reachings

118 Confronted with ancient mysteries, compounded by new doubts and uncertainties, modern Anglo-Saxon thinkers tend to adopt four broad strategies for dismissing them. They persist in the old rationalist/reductionist attempt to explain them away. Or they apply Wittgenstein's adroit veto on all further speculation: 'Whereof one cannot speak thereof one must be silent.' Or they became 'godless theologians'. Or they fall back into some form of Christian revivalism and resurrect the ancient dogmas of Christian theology.

119 This section attempts to examine, and dispute, all four of these responses.

120 To the reductionist the mystery words *(73)* love, beauty, time … are either airy abstractions contrived for our mystification by poets and metaphysicians; or they are symbols for legitimate general ideas which can easily be reduced to their simpler and quite unmysterious constituents.

121 Thus the apparently mysterious conduct of the hero, the lover and the reformed rake *(76-80)* can all be explained by reducing the motives and purposes of these men to those 'basic' and natural instincts which we share with the other animals.

122 In these terms, 'to fall in love' *(90)* is nothing more than a sophisticated but transparent device for selecting a mate.

123 Or it is seen as a socially-imposed smoke-screen which we emit in order to conceal from ourselves and others the aggressive lust of the male for the female; the female's lust for the male, intensified by her innate urge to become a mother.

124 As for the supposedly noble behaviour of those who give their lives for others *(76; 77; 80)*, the extreme reductionists still insist that we must see these heroes as conditioned creatures who continue to act according to socially- and family-imposed behaviour patterns even in situations where these patterns are no longer appropriate.

125 Or it is suggested that we were all so much in awe of our fathers as early exemplars of moral authority that we have transformed them into an interior psychological force (the Superego) which continues to issue imperative orders to us even when the father is far away or long dead.

126 As for the intense emotions engendered in us by the creation or the reception of the arts *(87-89; 92)*, these have been supplied with a wide variety of naturalistic explanations. They, too, have been described as sublimations of the sexual instinct.

127 They have also been attributed to a taste for order and harmony which the human race has acquired, over the millennia, in its slow and necessary introduction of order and harmony into its private and social relationships.

128 Others have postulated a correspondence between human physiology and artistic enjoyment. (At its simplest: our bodies can function only by 'observing' certain laws of stability and regularity; therefore our minds take pleasure in the stability and regularity inherent in art.)

129 As for the so-called 'problems of philosophy' *(46-48)*, many positivists – though more among scientists than among professional philosophers – still believe that most of these have been either solved or shown to be pseudo-problems. (Free-will and determinism? Our belief in our own freedom is no more than a useful – perhaps even a necessary – illusion, which enables us to ignore the bleak and enervating reality of a wholly-determined universe.)

130 (One recent Cambridge philosopher even denied his whole subject, on the grounds that to ask a philosophical question is nothing more nor less than the symptom of a particular neurosis. The questioner should at once be conducted, not to the study or the debating-hall, but to the consulting-room. The gratifying name of this witty and entertaining reductionist is John Wisdom.)

131 So-called mystical experience has, of course, received the same sort of treatment. Much play, for example, has been made with the erotic imagery often devised by mystics when they try to describe their visionary experiences to those who have never shared them.

132 (Freud coined the term 'the oceanic feeling' to describe all forms of mystical experience, as if by inventing a new

47

term he was somehow contriving to diminish or explain away that ancient and bewildering phenomenon.)

133 As for the anti-common-sense reports now being delivered by certain scientists (38-41; 51-62), reductionists are liable to display one of two distinct but related reactions to these embarrassments. The first is to say that physicists and astronomers are indeed talking literal nonsense at this particular time, but that further researches will assuredly return them to the fold of traditional common-sensical discourse.

134 The other reductionist strategy is to admit that our present conception of common sense may well be in need of expansion and emendation; but *eventually* our minds will be able to accept a universe of 'big bangs' and 'black holes' as easily as we now accept and understand the universe devised for the bewilderment of our ancestors by Galileo, Copernicus and Newton.

135 No doubt our reaction to this type of reductionist explanation will depend to a very large extent on our temperamental inclinations. There are certainly many thoughtful people who are perfectly satisfied with these interpretations. Others are confident that even if present reductionist arguments seem naive and inadequate, more sophisticated and satisfying versions will eventually emerge.

136 But there are others who find something *radically* inadequate about these attempts to reduce what they regard as the Higher to mere projections and elaborations of what they persist in regarding as the Lower.

137 Reductionists have no right whatever to assume that this dissatisfaction is due only, or principally, to an unregenerate yearning for the intoxications of high thinking, or to a cowardly refusal to face the bleak but ineluctable facts of determinism.

138 The serious and enduring objection to reductionism is simply that it involves a betrayal of fundamental empiricist precepts.

139 A great many non-mystics – and *all* those who lay claim to visionary experience of any kind – insist that this type of interpretation gives a ludicrously inadequate description of the phenomenon that they themselves have seen and felt and known.

140 How many lovers *while they are in love* have been able to accept the proposition that the experience they are encountering is nothing more, or better, than a sublimation of their sexual drive?

141 Who, in the throes of artistic ecstasy, whether creative or receptive, can believe himself to be enjoying a substitute orgasm?

142 As for the mystics – and these are far and away the most coherent and impressive body of witnesses – not one of them has ever accepted that his experience *could have been* either hallucinatory or compensatory. Indeed what they tell us is that the reality they have been made aware of during their visionary states is infinitely more real than the reality of everyday living.

143 It is true, of course, that people often misinterpret their own experiences. *But the experiencers are always the primal witnesses*, and their testament is of immeasurably greater value, *a priori*, than any interpretation which others may choose to put on it.

144 Is it not, indeed, a gross intellectual impropriety to reject a body of evidence simply on the grounds that it does not conform to our own preconceptions or experience? (This comes close to the cardinal philosophical sin of solipsism – the treatment of one's own experience as the only form which can be real, or valid, for oneself.)

145 The sin is all the more heinous when the awkward witnesses are known to be men and women of exceptional probity and good sense.

146 It is as if Captain Cook had returned to England and reported the existence of a great southern continent, only to be told by those who had stayed at home that he was certainly suffering from an illusion, due to the Captain's inordinate love of his mother; or to his social origins; or to his drunkenness; or to sea-sickness; or simply to his passionate *desire* to make a great discovery (wish-fulfilment).

147 Perhaps a closer analogy is that of a blind man who devotes the whole of his life to a (literally) benighted explanation of why it is that so many people are under the illusion that they 'see' things.

148 But there are two further arguments against reduction-

50

ism. The first is that it invariably confuses the occasion of an event with its sufficient cause. If a door opens and we suddenly see a view of distant mountains, it is true that we would not have seen the mountains unless the door had opened. But we would think it very odd if someone were to describe the opening of the door as the *cause* of the mountains; or even as the cause of our seeing them. It is plain enough that if there were no sexual instinct there would be no falling in love; but the transfiguration experienced by the lover is no more caused by his or her genitals than the mountains were caused by the opening of the door.

149 Another reductionist error is to believe that when you have discovered the embryonic form of a phenomenon you have also discovered an 'explanation' of it. As if the acorn 'explains' the oak tree!

150 Indeed it begins to seem that all those brash waves of reductionism have dashed themselves in vain against the eroded cliffs of love and art, of mystical vision and human nobility.

151 Consider, for a moment, two comparatively new words and their present associations: consider the word 'ethics' and the word 'aesthetics'. Why is it that the first sounds like a dry pea rattling in a dead pod? Why is it that the second has such an incurably spurious ring to it; as if of something fruitily oracular, almost irremediably pretentious?

152 'The greatest good of the greatest number.' 'That mode of behaviour which best conforms to the fullest and highest demands of human nature.' Does anyone still

believe that these empty tautologies can make any but the most marginal contribution to our understanding of a great and noble human action?

153 As for aesthetics, what can we feel, in our time, about its proliferation of so many fanciful and ephemeral manifestations: noble simplicity; life enhancement; significant form; objective correlative; social significance ... It is not that these terms have never been any use to us: it is simply that every one of them seems to leave the central core of the experience as untouched and mysterious as ever.

154 The error, perhaps, is that each of these very undisciplined 'disciplines' has been confusedly aspiring to the status of a science. Yet there is not, and by the nature of things there never can be, a science of value. (A fact which positivist philosophers have eagerly repeated at least since the time of Hume.)

155 The second main procedure of the irritable reachers after fact and reason is to maintain that although reductionists' arguments may fail, they do so only because they, no less than religious or absolutist arguments, have misunderstood the true relationship of language to experience. There are indeed limits to the capacity of mind: these precisely, and by definition, coincide with the limits to the capacity of language.

156 This seems a much more sophisticated – and conclusive – strategy than the devious endeavours of the reductionists. For it is surely the height of good sense, and good usage, to say that when you have reached the limits of what is

humanly conceivable, you must also have reached the limits of what is humanly expressible.

157 For the Inconceivable-Mysterious-Unanswerable is not, after all, a flesh-and-blood monster, against which we may continue to tilt with our lances and verbal description and analysis. To think otherwise is to make the same mistake that the King made in *Through the Looking Glass* when he envied Alice her ability to see Nobody when he himself couldn't even see real people in the bad light.

158 For such sternly self-denying philosophers the only legitimate use for such words as 'inconceivable' and 'inexpressible' is as terminal markers which register the limits of 'meaningful discourse'.

159 Yet this tidy full-stop is an even greater offence against empiricism than the – at least laborious and ingenious – explanations of the reductionists.

160 Wittgenstein's full proposition is as follows: 'What can be said at all can be said clearly: and whereof one cannot speak thereof one must be silent.'

161 Yet the first part of this famous declaration is as clearly untrue as it is clearly stated. Everyone has had experiences for which vague, muddled and confused language has seemed far less falsifying than a contrived precision and clarity.

162 And what they tell us – the lovers and art-lovers, the poets and the mystics – is that they have gone far beyond

the limits of what can be said clearly. They say that they have penetrated into a realm – or order, or continuum – which is so far outside the natural order that all attempts to describe it always fail. *But the failure is not complete.*

163 The true empiricist will recognize that the mysterious is *not* simply another word for the inexpressible. And that Wittgenstein's silence is therefore an evasion of the empiricist's obligation towards *the whole* of human experience. (Unless, as some have supposed and as other statements of Wittgenstein's suggest – see below – he meant that there is indeed a genuine order of religious experience, but that adequate words can never be found to describe it.)

164 Godless theology has the same sort of plausible simplicity about it as Wittgenstein's device, though it has proved to be an immeasurably brasher and more unprofitable enterprise.

165 Seldom can so many words have been used to say so little. For since not only God but the whole supernatural order has been abandoned, these self-styled theologians have simply turned themselves into amateur psychologist-philosophers who breathlessly repeat old rationalist propositions as if they had just invented them. (And why is it more helpful or informative to describe Our Ultimate Concern as 'God' than to describe it as our ultimate concern?)

166 The attempt to keep the trappings of theology while discarding the whole of its substance is perhaps the most barren intellectual exercise of our time.

167 The fourth procedure of those who are 'hot for certainties in this our life' is to fall back on some form of Christian revivalism. Of all the forms we know, by far the most sophisticated and intellectually imposing has been the biblicist neo-orthodoxy of Karl Barth.

168 Against the liberal-modernist reduction of God to some sort of faculty or aspiration within the human mind Barth firmly put him back in his heaven. Barth's God is at an infinite distance from man, and his only contact with his creatures is through his revealed Word in the New and Old Testaments, supplemented by the inspired dogmatics of the early Fathers. Thus the whole body of orthodox theology was restored to its previous unquestionable eminence.

169 But even Barth himself had begun to modify this extreme revivalism many years before his death. And in our own time that whole impressive and once-influential construction seems to have undergone a singular process of evaporation.

170 The plain fact is that the language and the religious thought of fourth-century Alexandria and Antioch are largely inappropriate to the speculative gropings of twentieth-century London and New York.

171 The historian can actually observe human ingenuities at work in the formulation of the creeds. And the argument against the capacity of such creeds to embody 'ultimate' truth is the argument against the ultimate nature of any truths arrived at by ratiocination alone – namely that the analytical/dialectical intellect can tell us only about facts and figures in the natural world. (We should – we must – use reason up to the very limits of its proper territory; it becomes a stultifying and misleading instrument whenever we try to use it beyond those limits.)

172 This is not to say that our language is better at answering difficult questions than the Greek of the fourth century. Indeed it might be said that our long habituation to positivist, scientific and analytical discourse has impoverished, even atrophied, our general speculative faculties. All we are now saying is that our own language happens to be the only one we have.

173 (It should be added, however, that there has never been a historical case in which a major system of belief has been widely discarded, only to make a triumphant subsequent return. In this respect such systems resemble all superannuated prima donnas.)

174 Within the terms of *our* thought and language you blaspheme against a mystery whenever you decorate, or inject, it with unwarranted naturalistic fantasies. And today the ancient disputes between Arians and Athanasians read like an infantile impertinence. *Our* necessary caution may not give a more truthful result than *their* flamboyant theological inventiveness. But in this territory of the almost-inexpressible, all that each generation can do is to devise a set of metaphors, old and new, which shall be appropriate to its own time and understanding.

175 In fact the attempt to revive obsolete dogmas and certitudes might be described as reductionism wearing a different suit of clothes. Our new intellectual and spiritual

predicament is just as unhelpfully over-simplified by re-course to an abandoned faith as our traditional perplexities have been over-simplified by sceptical reductionism.

176 None of these old theological contraptions seems to make any real contact with the core of mystical experience.

FOUR

Negative Capability

177 If the fault of the reductionists and the orthodox theologians is to be over-confident and over-explicit, the fault of the linguistic philosophers and the godless theologians is to give up too soon; to close their minds instead of keeping them open to further possibilities both of experience and of expression.

178 It was not only Keats who recommended a state of attentive and patient openness of mind, a refusal to reach irritably after fact and reason in a period, and a domain, where *nothing* can be said with the clarity which Wittgenstein once demanded.

179 The great message of Simone Weil is that we must *wait on* God, resisting the temptation to jump down into the ancient trenches and fortifications of dogma. But she also insisted that we must do this waiting in a state of positive and unremitting attention.

180 After Keats and before Weil, Meredith had shown us the other side of the coin:

> Ah, what a dusty answer gets the soul
> When hot for certainties in this our life.

181 In other passages Wittgenstein showed a more obviously respectful attitude towards that realm of human experience which lies beyond the reach of clear description:

'Even if *all possible* scientific questions be answered, the problems of life have still not been touched at all.'

182 Therefore nothing in this section will be either a supposedly self-evident axiom or a demonstrable theorem. We are no longer in the realm of reason and rational disputation; though we are still, and must always remain, in the realm of human experience.

183 It has been seen that there are many forms of 'other-worldly' experience, many occasions for that sense of an intangible, invisible and scarcely describable reality *beyond* the natural world of the senses; but it is plain that the full mystical vision is felt to be by far the most significant and enlightening of them all. Those who have known the transports of love and art but who have afterwards become capable of self-directed mystical experience are universally agreed that this later state both included and transcended all the others.

184 Therefore it is mystical experience in this fullest sense which makes the most urgent – as well as the most puzzling – demand on our attention.

185 If we believe that the descriptions and interpretations given by the mystics themselves are more to be trusted than those which have been so readily provided by others, then we must try to see whether anything useful can still be said about that experience. (This is a rash enterprise, of course, for the topic is hardly a new one.)

186 (Because we belong to the West we shall not be tempted to denounce the phenomenal world as 'unreal' and

'illusory' simply because we believe that there is another order of reality which is experienced as 'more real' than this one.)

187 From the nature of the case it seems likely that the greatest difficulty here will be the difficulty of language.

188 We constantly use metaphor in our everyday speech, but we use it legitimately only in cases where we can, if challenged, translate the metaphor back into a more literal and prosaic language. The purpose of metaphor in normal usage is to enhance, decorate, deepen, dignify, mock ... some proposition which might have been presented un-adorned.

189 The difficulty – some would say the absurdity – of trying to write about the meta-physical realm is that because we can talk about it in no language other than the meta-phorical, we can *never* deliver a literal equivalent but only offer, if challenged, an alternative metaphor.

190 Therefore the language we have to use in this near-inexpressible area of human experience is at the very opposite extreme from the order of language which used to be demanded by positivist philosophers. *Nothing* that is said here can be either verified or falsified, not even 'in principle'.

191 It is a ghostly language; a language of hint and suggestion, of echo and paradox: something much closer to the untranslatable communications of music than to the demonstrations of logic.

192 Indeed the major error of all schematic theologies has been their attempt to use a non-metaphorical language in an area where nothing but metaphor is appropriate. (Nor does their present retreat into metaphor alter the fact that the terms for which they now find so many ingenious interpretations were originally meant to be taken as literal and definitive statements.)

193 Theology used to describe itself as the Queen of the Sciences: it might have done better if it had tried to be the Queen of the Arts.

194 But although the formulations of the fourth century are no longer apt to our own far more doubtful and uncertain era, it would be absurd to deprive ourselves of the whole Christian vocabulary on the assumption that we must, at all costs, make a fresh start. Of all the forms and branches of human speech, the religious has the oldest and the noblest ancestry.

195 What is more, this ancient vocabulary acquires a patina, a depth of association, an accumulated force and mystery, which is peculiarly apt to any attempted description of a reality which lies, according to all reports, far outside our normal conception of time and history. (Words that are two thousand years old are eternal, of course, only by analogy; but analogies are all about us here.)

196 The question to be asked, in every case, is whether the traditional word or phrase seems to be exhausted by too long a burden of special meaning; or whether its long and hallowed use atones in reverberance for what it suffers in fatigue.

197 Since the early Fathers, the central doctrine of the church has been the Trinity: which implies, of course, the attendant doctrine of the Incarnation.

198 In our time it may well seem that there is nothing more barrenly formalistic than this concept of a trinitarian God: nothing more arid than the history of those early councils which formulated the doctrine with so much semantic dexterity and so many ferocious periphrastic disputations.

199 It has been suggested *(17-22)* that we can no longer believe in the first person of the Trinity (fatherly Creator-God) because we find his created universe an abomination of unnecessary cruelty. (Besides, what is the concept of God the Creator but the anthropomorphic for *homo faber*?)

200 But what of the second person? What of 'christology', the most-favoured jargon-term in the whole vocabulary of modern theology? It is plain that a good many Christian apologists, whether neo-orthodox or ultra-modernist, have retreated into that inner keep of their once-gigantic and complex castle where they can at least continue to discourse on the person and nature of Jesus Christ. It is here, supremely if not uniquely, that we are to find God still working in the world — whatever 'God' may be. ('Christology' has begun to sound as arid as 'ethics', as fulsome as 'aesthetics'.)

201 But we are bound to reject Jesus of Nazareth as the second person of the Trinity not only because the continued dissection of his nature now seems like a piece of almost frivolous antiquarianism, but also because this doctrine is the most naively anthropomorphic of them all.

202 Apart from the intrinsic egocentricity of supposing that the reality beyond our own must contain something resembling ourselves (though bigger and better), there is another and a new factor which militates strongly against the concept of a God who is one-third man. Scientific explorers of the natural universe now believe that it may contain many millions of intelligent life-forms, of which some, at least, must surely be more advanced than our own. (Imagine a creature – or suppose one, anyway – which is equipped with twice as many senses as we have; no supposition makes more evidently absurd the assumption that reality ends at the furthest reach of our own five senses.)

203 Why, then, should this particular race on this particular planet have been chosen for the unique privilege of constituting a third part of the Universal Godhead?

204 (Reflecting on the old concepts of God the Father and God the Son it may well seem that the word 'God' has itself been so heavily burdened with anthropomorphic implications that we can no longer safely use it without misleading ourselves and others. But this rejection of an old and honoured term is a very different thing from the comprehensive jettisoning of the whole supernatural order by the death-of-God 'theologians'.)

205 So all that remains of the Christian Trinity is its most mysterious and subordinate member: that Holy Ghost or Holy Spirit which was described, at long last, as 'proceeding from the Father *and the Son*'. Is *this*, perhaps, a term which combines the inherited value of long, and certainly hallowed, use with our modern need for religious meta-

phors which are vague yet evocative, loose in meaning but forceful in suggestion?

206 A scientific hypothesis is a proposed form of words or symbols which will be provisionally accepted if, and only if, it enables further investigations to be more effectively pursued.

207 The gulf between religious and scientific procedures is very wide; as wide as the different languages they use. But they have at least this in common, that a proposed form of words can be tested only by its effectiveness as a new instrument of communication, and by its capacity to assist more fruitful formulations in the future.

208 It is suggested here that the term 'Holy Spirit' – sharply severed from its previous associates – will continue to be a vital factor in any contemporary discussion of religious experience. (It may also seem that this capacious term can embrace and illuminate all those lesser visions which come to us through love and art, through the spectacle of courage, self-sacrifice and regeneration.)

209 Certainly it is a term which allows us to remain in that condition of patient openness which was recommended to us by Keats, Weil and Meredith. For nothing is *specified* by the old term, although so much is suggested and invoked.

210 To begin as dryly as we may: the Holy Spirit is a supra-personal force, experienced both as personal and as non-personal, which exists outside the natural order and independently of any human or other mind, but which also operates with and through the mind. (Sometimes the

initiative is felt to be coming from the mind itself, a striving towards the Spirit; sometimes there is a sense of involuntary invasion, penetration, suffusion of the mind by the Holy Spirit.)

211 Can we shore up a disintegrating term like the word 'soul' by defining it as that part of the mind which reaches out to, and is reached out to by, the Holy Spirit?

212 What seems to be clear from all mystical reports is that it is not the reasoning and calculating element in the mind which is able to make contact with the Spirit. 'Where the mind fails,' writes the author of the *Cloud of Unknowing*, 'love becomes the only way forward.' This is to say that in the matter of mystical communication, love is no longer only a virtue: it is also a faculty.

213 Faith and hope seem to be faculties of the same order: faith not as a blind belief in the incredible but as the capacity for a trusting openness towards the Holy Spirit. Hope as a persistent trust in the sacred experience of others even while our own continues to be meagre; or less than meagre.

214 (But none of this implies that the rational intellect is somehow degraded or dishonoured. It is a proper, even a sacred, element in all our normal activities and communications on earth. The Holy Spirit cannot be anti-rational: it must include and transcend the whole of the rational.)

215 The man who prays for the descent of the Spirit without any apparent result should recognize that his religious faculty may be *inherently* weak, much as some people are born with a 'bad ear' or a poor capacity for visual enjoy-

ment. (On the other hand, someone who is bad at praying may find that he is receiving the Holy Spirit through other – perhaps long familiar – means. He may be one of those for whom daily life itself provides the sacramental occasion; the moment of at least half-visionary illumination.)

216 New phrases also have their uses. We might describe the Holy Spirit – in undiminished awareness that every description always fails – as a mental continuum. Certainly it seems, from all the reports, to be much more like a state than a thing: more like a function of experience than a place; at least as much a force as a person.

217 Just as our world seems to be based on the primacy of matter, so the world of the Spirit seems to be based on the primacy of mind. And just as the mind usually 'proceeds from' matter in the material world, so it may be that spirit proceeds from mind on the next level of reality. (We have no reason for supposing that even on our own level, mind can function *only* in association with matter. Many mystics, and others, have experienced a temporary separation of the mind from the body.)

218 So what we must now try to contemplate is a Spirit-Mind which never did or could 'create' the natural world, but which has always brooded over that world, seeking for means to penetrate and influence it.

219 We may suppose that a prime function of the Holy Spirit has been to vitalize dead matter; then to mentalize primitive life; at last to spiritualize the earthbound mind. Thus some, at least, of the absurdities inherent in evolutionary theories *(60-62)* are modified, even removed.

220 Of course it is true, and has often been said, that devices of this kind only move the mystery of origins back a stage. But it is a very important stage. For instead of stubbornly insisting on an autonomous and naturalistic account of matter turning into mind, we can now suppose a pre-existent (and eternal?) mind working – perhaps with the utmost difficulty – on the hard and recalcitrant substance of the world. *We have moved the mystery back into that area which is (for us) wholly and properly composed of mysteries.*

221 (This does nothing, of course, to help us with the mystery of the origins of matter. But this, too, lies in the area of our *inevitable* bewilderment.)

222 We might say that evolution has been a process of pulling rather than pushing, and the final end/purpose/ endeavour of the Holy Spirit is to spiritualize the whole of the phenomenal universe. (We must think teleologically at least as much as we now think aetiologically.)

223 In this light we should see ourselves as potential helpers or hinderers of the Spirit in its inconceivable task. And in this light, what we do, or fail to do, is of crucial importance – as it could not possibly be if we were the puppets of an omnipotent and omniscient Creator-God. We were not created for the amusement of a God who knew from the beginning exactly what our end would be. We were drawn out of base matter because the mind of men, and of all other intelligent beings, is indispensable to that great task of the Holy Spirit which the mind itself can only glimpse, guess at and stutter about.

224 Certainly we find very little in the writings of the

mystics to suggest that the Holy Spirit is encountered as a Creator- and Sustainer-God who wills and directs the fall of every leaf and sparrow. (Earthquakes [23] are no more willed or caused by the Holy Spirit than they are willed or caused by man: most of matter seems to remain intractable both to man and to the Spirit.)

225 The Barthian fallacy was to suppose a God infinitely removed from man and the world: this was a theory of total transcendence.

226 The pantheist fallacy was to suppose that the Holy Spirit dwells only in and through the order of nature: this was a theory of total immanence.

227 A renewed concept of the Holy Spirit eminently conforms to the ancient religious perception of a supernatural order which both penetrates and remains distinct from the natural order.

228 (Any attempt to revive a hallowed religious concept is a reminder of how much light we can still find in all the great religious classics – from Second Isaiah to Simone Weil; from Buddha to Ramakrishna.)

229 We should always keep in mind the notion of extrapolation: of the visible graph-line which ends in the right-hand top corner of the paper; of human actions and experiences which seem to us, and often so forcibly, like rudimentary versions of something higher and more complete.

230 To accord with this strong and repeated impression, we might say that the Holy Spirit is *always* present, however

imperceptibly, in every human soul; and that these portions – envoys? – create within us a longing for the fullness of the Spirit in all its love and glory.

231 It is possible, in these terms, to reinterpret old words without changing their essential and hallowed meaning. Thus heaven is that state in which the Holy Spirit is most fully and perceptibly present in a human soul; absolute hell is an inability to discover any gleam of the Spirit's light either inside the soul or in the world outside.

232 What has been described as an 'age of faith' may indeed be a period of history when, for reasons beyond the obvious historical ones, the Holy Spirit permeated our world with unusual profusion and effect.

233 The guardian angel becomes a brilliant and touching acknowledgment of the fact that some people are clearly more blessed than others with the surveillance and suffusion of the Spirit. Thus although it no longer seems helpful to describe Jesus as the second person of the Trinity, we can readily understand that this wonderful and astonishing man was suffused by the Spirit to an extraordinary degree. (It is tempting, but surely too parochial, to describe that particular action of the Spirit as historically unique.)

234 According to many reports from returned travellers, the Holy Spirit is seldom experienced as *more complex* than the natural world. In contrast to our own multiple and heterogeneous order, the Spirit seems to be of an inconceivable simplicity, purity and integrity ...

235 And so each one of us might continue to add jot-

tings, hints and metaphors deriving from the reports of our betters; tentative forms of words devised to communicate some minor experiences of our own.

236 It does not seem irrational, superstitious or beyond our means to speak of the Holy Spirit and to pray for the Spirit's descent on ourselves and on our world.

237 But far more important than any phrase or formulation, however rich in association and restored significance, is the capacity to wait in a state of attention, cultivating the attentive faculties of love, hope and faith, resisting as best we can that heat for certainty which seems to be one of our strongest impulses and a principal cause of our most constant errors and afflictions.

POSTSCRIPT

A Marriage of Heaven and Earth

1 The full array of orthodox Christianity has been a splendid and inspiriting body of doctrine. And if this faith is now dying to be born again, the emergent phoenix must shine at least as brightly and transformingly as the old one used to do.

'Glory to glory, as by the spirit of the Lord.'

2 And like every new Christian exploration this one must turn back yet again to the New Testament and find in that undimmed constellation yet a new pattern of signs and proclamations.

3 Reading those too-familiar books again I have begun to think that I see something hinted at there, and nearly spoken aloud, which may have been missed by other readers, and which might, by one of those slight shifts of vision, reilluminate the word and give a new Christian message to our time.

4 The earliest recorded Israelites had understood God in the image of their Most Admired Man. At that time this meant any great king or emperor who had carved out a great dominion for himself; who ruled it with beneficence towards those who humbled themselves before him, but with terrible anger against all who resisted or denied him.

5 But a new kind of God had been gradually softening the harsh lines of the old one; and what Jesus nearly did, by his

recorded words, his life and death, was to proclaim this new vision of God as a total transcendence of Jahweh, the tribal tyrant of Israel.

6 Yet what was left to the world, according to the traditional interpretation of the New Testament, is like a sublime statue half-emerging from a great block of rough-hewn granite. Because Jesus was himself a believing Jew; because he suffered from an anger which could distort his marvellous vision; perhaps because his words were misunderstood even by his closest disciples, the Christian Churches inherited a concept of God which is centaur-like in its weird inconsonance.*

7 The traditional God of Christianity has been that same old Emperor-Creator, but one who also loves his creature-subjects as a father loves his children. Thus the problem of evil has bedevilled the Christian faith at least since the age of Augustine and Pelagius. This ancient conundrum of a God who is both all-powerful and all-loving has become even more acute both as men have learned more about the physical universe and also as they have come to regard cruelty as the worst of all human – and *a fortiori* of divine – abominations.

8 We have been told that an all-powerful, all-loving Creator-God has made a world of earthquakes and meningitis; of Belsen and Hiroshima; – a world which has reached its present state after the brutal, billion-year tale of the fittest so savagely surviving.

* All this may seem a blasphemous impertinence; but there is an old image of the pygmy who sits on a giant's shoulders and sees a few yards more of the great landscape discovered by the giant's mighty vision.

78

9 Almost every modern theologian has tried to solve this problem; but it can never be solved until one of the contradictory terms is removed. What was so nearly revealed in the New Testament, what can be seen there now in brilliant but elusive outline, is *a God who does not possess two distinct attributes called 'power' and 'love', but a God whose power lies only and wholly in his love.*

10 A believable God must always be an extrapolation from the most admired of men, for we see such men as true manifestations of God. In our own time all Christians, and all those non-believers who still live in the moral ambience of Christianity, are agreed that Jesus is more to be admired than Augustus; St Francis than Genghiz Khan; the Curé d'Ars than Napoleon. Yet most Christians still try to worship a God who is half Genghiz Khan and half St Francis.

11 And even if the Jesus of the New Testament is not a sinless man – his terrible rages against all who would not accept him are all-too-human – the essential message of his words, his life and his death is that love triumphs not only over all physical power but even over death itself. (We have tended to treat St Paul's great passage in his First Letter to the Corinthians as the natural hyperbole of a poet. But it is literally true, even in this world, that love is the only enduring power, since it is the only power which is not ultimately self-defeating.)

12 All Christians believe that God was made manifest in Jesus Christ: many Christians still believe that God *was* Jesus Christ. But Jesus not only exercised no physical or political power; he treated the offer of such power as a

temptation by the devil. Can anyone believe that the Father revels in what the Son so scornfully rejected?

13 Every theology is a mythology and must have new stories to tell.

14 This story begins in that total ignorance of all origins which most physicists and astronomers now confess to. And the story itself is taken up where the scientists first begin to make persuasive guesses. The earth is thrown off the sun: it cools: life begins in the ocean: life evolves on land and culminates – so far – in man.

15 But those who believe that this is a summary of the *whole* story are surely confronted by the exact converse of the problem which has tormented so many orthodox believers for so many centuries. Rationalists, materialists and atheists have never yet fully faced the *Problem of Good*.

16 If man had been the product of natural evolution alone he would indeed be a naked ape: all his superb intelligence would be directed only to the survival of his own species in a state of maximum pleasure and minimum pain. He would differ from the other animals *only* by the higher degree of his intelligence.

17 The best we could ever expect would be a society conforming to some old blueprint drawn up by Sidney and Beatrice Webb – a community organized with the maximum intelligence to provide the greatest possible physical and mental satisfaction for all its members.

18 There would be no art in such a society, for art always

implies a dissatisfaction with given reality. There would be no religion, for religion is always the yearning for an unachieved condition – of love, of wisdom, of illumination. Men and women would be united by bonds of enlightened self-interest, but there would be no love between them: for love leads to the pains of separation; to the ultimate anguish of bereavement.

19 Why, then, has such a 'utopia' never been achieved? Why would most human beings reject it with horror if it were offered them? Why do men hunger so irrepressibly for love, for beauty, for truth? At least *for struggle*? Why does the totally supererogatory goodness of Jesus or St Francis continue to captivate the imagination even of those who cannot believe in the God of Jesus and St Francis? *Where* did Jesus and the saints find that sublime love which would not only be superfluous in a naked ape but deeply destructive of his super-simian contentment?

20 'Naturalistic' interpretations of Jesus or St Francis, of St John of the Cross or St Teresa do not seem blasphemous or even disrespectful. Such accounts of these figures never get near the reality of those extraordinary lives; they seem grotesque in their irrelevance. It is as if someone had given an account of a great picture by a careful description of all its shapes and colours.

21 So this theological story tells of something outside our universe, and of a different kind from it, which is constantly pressing in upon our domain of the senses and trying to introduce the freedom of the spirit into an order of rigorous material necessity.

22 When we think of this 'something other' as a force, a state or a domain we call it heaven; when we think of it as a person we call it God. And just as physicists treat light either as waves or particles according to context, so we talk either of God or of heaven as it suits us. Yet we are *always* fully aware that whatever words we use will be no better than pointing fingers; gestures of dumb joy; grimaces of bewildered love.

23 One model might be a black and hollow globe surrounded by radiant light: whenever the smallest chink appears in the surface of our globe the light *will* enter, of its very nature. Or we may think of a wise and loving father or mother who is constantly offering strange and inestimable gifts to sons and daughters who seldom even hear the parental voice, and still more rarely open their hearts and minds to receive what is being offered.

24 The present story tells us that as evolution proceeds, on this or any other planet, so God enters the expanding minds of thinking beings as best he can. (He may have other ways of entering our universe and influencing events here, but the only way we can hope to understand is the way he makes into our own minds.)

25 These divine gifts are prodigious and invaluable, for all of them are of heavenly origin and could not have been the products of any earthly process. The greatest gift is the gift of religious understanding, for this can enable us to receive as much of heaven's light as we are ever able to receive. Other gifts are inner freedom (for the natural world knows nothing but necessity); the knowledge of good and evil (for the natural world knows nothing but advantage and dis-

advantage); art; love; joyful perception of beauty in the uncreated world around us; ardour for truth; redeeming pain ... When we see, or feel, these gifts in action, surely they seem like mysterious colonists from some more splendid realm of being than our own?*

26 So the supreme function of men and women is to receive God's gifts, the light of heaven, as fully as they can. Some people are congenitally better attuned to the will of God, more permeable to heaven's light; but all of us can work continually to make ourselves more receptive – by encouraging whatever we can find in ourselves of faith and hope; by prayer and meditation; by reading; by self-attrition; by alert attention to even the most familiar and everyday experiences. But, above all, by practising the art of love. 'I am come that ye might have life and that ye might have it more abundantly.'

27 If it is hard to reach this God it is not because he coyly, or pedagogically, withdraws himself from us, but because it is as hard for him to penetrate our world as it is for us to receive the radiance of his love. For most of us God is an endless journey.

28 The tragedy of this life is in no way diminished by discovering a God of pure love, but the tragedy is not due to God's obscure purposes in tormenting us but to the hard fact that we are truly the creature-victims of a world ruled by unfeeling necessity. Yet the tragedy is now truly redeemable by the accessibility of God's *unequivocal* love.

* Thus God is indeed the creator *of man*, in the sense that he has given man everything which is of the least value in him, and everything which enables him to value truly.

29 Stupidity, blindness, folly and wickedness form a thick impasto around us through which God can scarcely reach us, even though his effort to do so is never relaxed. (This is clearly a God to whom the phrase 'Forgive us our sins' cannot be addressed with any meaning whatever! Our sins are forgiven as soon as they are committed; *before* they are committed. The problem for us is to penetrate our carapace of sinful egotism and recognize God's love as something which is always there; which can never be withdrawn.)

30 Many modern theologians have mocked the idea of 'a God out there', and many of them have ended up with the man-centred parochialism of suggesting that 'God' is simply another term for 'our deepest concern' or 'the depth of our being'.

31 But the present story, while reluctant to use such huge and hollow words as 'infinite' and 'eternal', records that God/heaven was there long before the arrival of man on earth, and will be there long after man's departure. (God may be latent within us all, but he can be brought into loving activity only by our worship of a God whose existence is in no way dependent on our own.)

32 But it seems futile to speculate about the intrinsic nature of God, and it was the tormented efforts of early theologians to do this which led them to create their forbidding structures of creed, dogma and anathema. New Testament Christianity scarcely concerns itself at all with the inner nature of God and heaven. The Gospels, Acts and most of the Epistles, Pauline or otherwise, are intensely concerned with the mystery of God's dealings with man as revealed

by the recorded words, life, death and resurrection of Jesus Christ.

33 The first two supplications of the supreme Christian prayer contain the heart of the whole proclamation. 'Thy kingdom come. Thy will be done in earth as it is in heaven.' For the kingdom is *not yet* come; God's will is *not yet* done on earth.

34 Indeed if we now read the New Testament in the light of the present story it is extraordinary how little needs to be surrendered; or even reinterpreted. And there are some great utterances which make *more* sense in the light of a God truly revealed by the life of Jesus; truly almighty in love alone. 'My grace is sufficient for you: my power is made perfect in weakness.' (If God were really a wielder of mighty physical power surely he would choose for his most favoured children those who most resemble him: not the weak, the poor and the humble but the great kings of the earth. But being himself a persistent suppliant on earth it is to the weak, the humble and the supplicating that he finds it easiest to come.)

35 The great heaven-sent utterances of the New Testament surely sound all the louder and clearer once we have banished that omnipotent Creator and omniscient Predestinator. 'Abide in me and I in you.' 'Perfect love casteth out fear.' 'The truth shall make you free.' 'Except a man be born again he cannot see the Kingdom of God.' 'Rise, thou that sleepeth, and arise from the dead; and Christ shall enlighten thee.' 'The words I speak unto you, they are spirit and they are life.' 'God is a spirit, and those that would come to him must come in spirit and in truth.'

'Where the spirit of the Lord is, there is liberty.' 'I am the Way, the Truth and the Life.' 'Seek and ye shall find.' 'Peace I leave with you, my peace I give unto you: not as the world giveth give I unto you.'

INDEX

References are to the numbered paragraphs; those in the Postscript are indicated by italics.